Madam C.J. Walker

The Woman Behind Hair Care Products for African Americans

by Sally Lee

PEBBLE
a capstone imprint

Little Explorer is published by Pebble,
1710 Roe Crest Drive, North Mankato, Minnesota 56003
www.capstonepub.com

The name of the Smithsonian Institution and the sunburst
logo are registered trademarks of the Smithsonian Institution.
For more information, please visit www.si.edu.

Library of Congress Cataloging-in-Publication Data is available on the Library of Congress website.
ISBN 978-1-9771-0971-2 (library binding)
ISBN 978-1-9771-1058-9 (paperback)
ISBN 978-1-9771-0981-1 (eBook PDF)

Summary: In the early 20th century, Madam C.J. Walker identified a problem, one she herself had: African
Americans had no hair care products specifically designed for their hair type. So what did she do? The
uneducated daughter of sharecroppers researched, invented, tested, refined, and marketed her way to
becoming a self-made millionaire! Historic photos fortify this inspiring rags-to-riches story.

Editorial Credits

Jill Kalz, editor; Kayla Rossow, designer; Svetlana Zhurkin, media researcher;
Tori Abraham, production specialist

Our very special thanks to Emma Grahn, Spark!Lab Manager, Lemelson Center for the Study of Invention
and Innovation, National Museum of American History. Capstone would also like to thank Kealy Gordon,
Product Development Manager, and the following at Smithsonian Enterprises: Ellen Nanney, Licensing
Manager; Brigid Ferraro, Vice President, Education and Consumer Products; and Carol LeBlanc, Senior
Vice President, Education and Consumer Products.

Image Credits

A'Lelia Bundles/Madam Walker Family Archives, cover (left), 5, 17, 18, 19, 28, 29 (top); Alamy: Interfoto,
7 (top), Old Paper Studios, 9; Indiana Historical Society: Madam C.J. Walker Collection, 22; Library of
Congress, 7 (bottom), 11, 13 (bottom), 14, 24, 25, 27; The New York Public Library, 10, 12, 13 (top),
20; Shutterstock: Igor Golovniov, 29 (bottom); Smithsonian Institution: Collection of the Smithsonian
National Museum of African American History and Culture, Gift from Dawn Simon Spears and Alvin
Spears, Sr., cover (right), 15, Collection of the Smithsonian National Museum of African American History
and Culture, Gift of A'Lelia Bundles/Madam Walker Family Archives, 16, 21, 23 (bottom), National
Museum of American History, 23 (top)

Design Elements by Shutterstock

All internet sites appearing in back matter were available and accurate when this book was sent to press.

Printed in the United States of America.
PA70

TABLE OF CONTENTS

INTRODUCTION

When you hear the word "inventor," who do you see? A rich white man? Most people do. But *anyone* can be an inventor! Success comes from good ideas and the willingness to work hard.

Madam C.J. Walker was an unlikely inventor. She was a young, poor, black woman, born soon after the Civil War. However, at the age of 37, she became a pioneer in the hair care and beauty industry. She invented a brand of hair care products for black women, became a millionaire, and inspired countless women around the world to follow their dreams.

The U.S. Civil War was fought from 1861 to 1865. It was between states in the North and states in the South. One result of the war was freedom for people who had been enslaved.

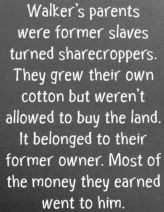

Walker's parents were former slaves turned sharecroppers. They grew their own cotton but weren't allowed to buy the land. It belonged to their former owner. Most of the money they earned went to him.

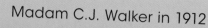

Madam C.J. Walker in 1912

DIFFICULT CHILDHOOD

Madam C.J. Walker was born in 1867 as Sarah Breedlove. She was the fifth of six children—the first born free. Her family lived on a cotton plantation in Louisiana. As a child Sarah picked cotton. She helped her mother wash clothes for others.

By the time Sarah was 7 years old, her parents died. She lived with her older sister for a while. But her sister's husband treated Sarah poorly.

Sarah dreamed of going to school, but she wasn't allowed. At that time many white people in the South didn't want black people to have an education. It was easier to control people who didn't know how to read and write.

When Sarah was a child, all cotton was picked by hand.

Doing laundry was hard work. Clothes were washed with harsh soaps in tubs of boiling water. The heavy, wet clothes were hung on lines to dry. Then they were pressed with irons heated on the stove.

A HOME OF HER OWN

Sarah needed to get away from her cruel brother-in-law. She wanted a home of her own. She got it by marrying Moses McWilliams. She was just 14 years old.

Three years later the couple had a daughter, Lelia. Sarah wanted to give Lelia a better life than she had. But Moses died soon after. Sarah became a single mother at age 20. She needed a new start. Sarah and Lelia moved to St. Louis, Missouri, in 1888.

After the Civil War, some people in the South were angry that the slaves had been freed. Many black people were terrorized. Many others were lynched.

Many black people in the South moved to St. Louis in the late 1800s. Jobs were easier to find there than other places in the South. Sarah's three brothers owned a barbershop in St. Louis.

St. Louis, Missouri, in 1890

LIFE IN ST. LOUIS

In the late 1800s, washing clothes was one of the few jobs available to women without an education.

Sarah worked hard washing clothes. It was the only job she knew. She worked six days a week. Sundays were for church.

Sarah was very active in her church. She and Lelia were members of the St. Paul African Methodist Episcopal Church in St. Louis.

Church not only gave people a place to pray, but it also was a place to share ideas and help one another.

Sarah saw many successful black women. She wanted to be like them. But she didn't know how. She later said, "As I bent over the washboard and looked at my arms buried in soapsuds, I said to myself, 'What are you going to do when you grow old and your back gets stiff? Who is going to take care of your little girl?'"

JIM CROW LAWS

Jim Crow laws began in the South in the 1880s. The laws kept black people from having the same freedoms that white people enjoyed. Black people were not allowed to go to the same schools, restaurants, and theaters as white people. They could not use the same bathrooms and drinking fountains. Most black people were not allowed to vote. Jim Crow laws were outlawed by the Civil Rights Act of 1964.

Sarah worked hard and saved her money. Sarah was able to send Lelia to college. Now it was time to help herself. Sarah went to night school to better her mind. She also wanted to improve her looks. Her hair was breaking off. Clumps were falling out.

In 1902 Sarah met Annie Pope Turnbo. Annie had a line of hair care products for black women, called Poro. She hired Sarah to sell the products for her door-to-door.

Annie Pope Turnbo

Many black women at that time had hair problems. Poor diets and harsh hair treatments were mostly to blame.

PORO
HAIR & BEAUTY
CULTURE

A world's fair was held in St. Louis in 1904. Many successful black women went to a meeting there. They believed in the words "Lifting as We Climb." They inspired Sarah to change her life.

People came to St. Louis for the World's Fair in 1904.

13

A FRESH START

In 1905 Sarah wanted a fresh start. She moved to Denver, Colorado. She worked hard cooking, washing clothes, and selling Poro products. Sarah liked the idea

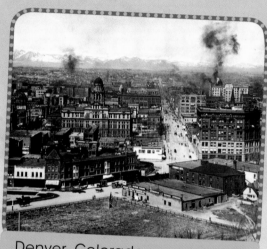

Denver, Colorado, around 1908

of hair care products for black women. Unfortunately the Poro products didn't work well on her own hair. She believed she could invent something that would.

Sarah began testing different ingredients. She tried, failed, and tried again. Finally she invented a mixture she liked. At age 37 Sarah started her own business.

STEPS TO INVENTION

Sarah knew black women needed better hair care products. She tried mixing different ingredients. She tested each mixture on herself and others. Some mixtures worked a little. Some didn't work at all. Sarah tried many times to get her product, called Wonderful Hair Grower, just right. Then she used these steps to invent more products. Sarah was successful because her products worked. She was also very good at selling them.

How did Sarah pick her ingredients? She said an African man came to her in a dream and gave her a list. Some people think she had help from a local pharmacist.

THE WALKER COMPANY

NATIONAL
CONVENTION
OF
MADAM
C.J. WALKER'S
AGENTS

The saleswomen of the Walker Company were called Walker Agents.

Sarah married C.J. Walker in 1906. She began using the name Madam C.J. Walker. Her new business was called the Walker Company.

Sarah and C.J. grew their business. She held events to show black women how to use her products. She hired sales agents. The Walker Company was special. It was created by black people to better the lives of black people. It provided jobs and education to thousands of black women.

Sarah used the French title "Madam" instead of "Mrs." It made people think of France, then the world capital of fashion and beauty.

WORKING HARDER

Walker's company grew quickly. Each month more orders came in. Business was booming! When Lelia finished college, she ran the company's mail-order service.

In the early 1900s, many white people thought black people weren't smart enough to run a business. They didn't think women were, either. Walker proved them wrong on both counts.

Like her mother, Lelia Walker was a strong businesswoman.

Walker and C.J. spent 18 months traveling to other states. Walker taught women about her hair care products. She hired and trained sales agents. By 1907 Walker was making more money than most white men.

Some people think Walker invented hot combs, which were used to make hair straighter. She didn't. But she did use them as part of her hair treatments.

Walker (seated, middle) and her sales agents

HEADING TO PITTSBURGH

In 1908 Walker and her family moved to Pittsburgh, Pennsylvania. The large city had 16 railroad lines. Those lines made it easy to ship out Walker's products.

In the early 1900s, Pittsburgh's Union Station was a hub of railroad activity.

The lack of education limited the jobs available to many black women. Children raised in poor conditions often had to work instead of going to school. Some areas had no schools for black people.

Walker used her success to help other black women. Most of them worked cleaning houses or doing laundry. Walker knew they were capable of doing more. She opened Lelia College to teach them the skills they needed to get better jobs.

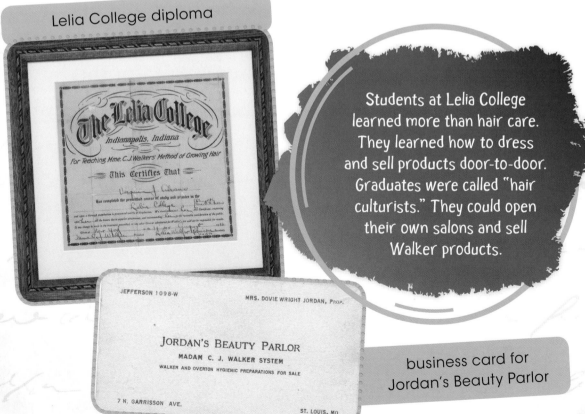

Lelia College diploma

The Lelia College
Indianapolis, Indiana
For Teaching Mme. C.J. Walkers' Method of Growing Hair
This Certifies That

Students at Lelia College learned more than hair care. They learned how to dress and sell products door-to-door. Graduates were called "hair culturists." They could open their own salons and sell Walker products.

JEFFERSON 1098-W   MRS. DOVIE WRIGHT JORDAN, PROP.

JORDAN'S BEAUTY PARLOR
MADAM C. J. WALKER SYSTEM
WALKER AND OVERTON HYGIENIC PREPARATIONS FOR SALE

7 N. GARRISSON AVE.   ST. LOUIS, MO.

business card for
Jordan's Beauty Parlor

ON THE MOVE AGAIN

Walker and C.J. moved to Indianapolis, Indiana, in 1910. The city had a well-developed black business community.

Walker's house was big enough for a small factory and a beauty salon. But her growing company needed more room. She built a larger factory. The business did very well. Walker's marriage, however, did not. Two years later she and C.J. divorced.

Walker in front of her home in Indianapolis, Indiana, around 1910

Glossine protected hair from the damage caused by hot combs.

WALKER'S GLOSSINE

MADE BY
THE MADAM C.J. WALKER
MANUFACTURING CO.
INDIANAPOLIS, IND.
PRICE 35 CTS.

FOR BEAUTIFYING AND SOFTENING THE HAIR.

When Indianapolis needed a new YMCA for black people, Walker donated $1,000. It was the most money given to the YMCA by any black person.

Walker believed in uplifting black people through education. She supported black schools and helped many students pay for college. She opened her own schools to train beauty consultants.

AUTHORIZED
AGENT

Wm. C.J. Walker's
SYSTEM AND PREPARATIONS

RESPECT

Booker T. Washington was an important black leader in the early 1900s. Walker wanted his respect. But he wouldn't let her speak to his business groups.

Booker T. Washington was born into slavery. He became a teacher and the head of the Tuskegee Institute, a college for black people. He also helped black businesses.

In 1912 Walker went to a meeting of the National Negro Business League. She stood up without being called on. "Surely you are not going to shut the door in my face," she said boldly. She told her story of going from the cotton fields to building a business. By the time she finished, she'd won over the entire group.

"I am a woman who came from the cotton fields of the South. From there I was promoted to the washtub. From there I was promoted to the cook kitchen. And from there I promoted myself into the business of manufacturing hair goods and preparations. . . . I have built my own factory on my own ground."
—Madam C.J. Walker, at the National Negro Business League Convention, July 1912

FIGHTING FOR HER RACE

Walker worked hard to improve the lives of black people. Many people could not afford food, housing, and health care. Walker donated money to groups that helped with those needs. She helped thousands of black women get better paying jobs. She also spoke out against unfair treatment of black people in general. Walker gave many people hope for a better life.

In 1916 Walker started a union for her agents. She asked them to speak out about unfair treatment of black people. She gave prizes to agents who did the most to help others.

The continuing violence against black people angered Walker. Lynchings were still common in the early 1900s. In 1917 she helped plan a march in New York City. Thousands of black people walked silently down Fifth Avenue to protest the violence.

In July 1917 a silent march in New York City protested the violence against black Americans.

Walker moved to New York City in 1916. Lelia had opened a fancy gathering place there. Walker worked hard and enjoyed New York's parties and events.

A couple of years later, she left the bustle of the city. She built a mansion on the Hudson River in Irvington, New York. The grand home shocked neighbors. They couldn't believe that a black woman owned it.

A gathering of Walker's sales agents at her home in 1924

Walker kept working, even when her health failed. "I want to live to help my race," she told her doctor. Madam C.J. Walker died on May 25, 1919. She was 51 years old.

In 1998 the U.S. Postal Service honored Walker. They put her picture on a stamp. It was part of their Black Heritage series.

29

GLOSSARY

agent—a person who has the right to do certain actions for another person

donate—to give something as a gift

harsh—having a bad or harmful effect

ingredient—one of the things that are used to make a food or product

inspire—to cause someone to want to do something positive

inventor—a person who thinks up and makes something new

lynch—to be put to death by a mob without a trial, usually by hanging

orphanage—a home for children whose parents have died

pharmacist—a person who is allowed to prepare and sell medicine

pioneer—a person who is one of the first to try new things

plantation—a large farm found in warm areas; before the Civil War, plantations in the South used slave labor

protest—a strong, public gathering of people who want something to be changed

respect—a deep belief in someone's abilities or worth

sharecropper—a farmer who raises crops for a land owner and is paid some of the money from the sale of the crop

terrorize—to make people fearful by using actions meant to cause injury, pain, or harm

treatment—something that you use, or something you do, to feel and look healthy or attractive

violence—actions meant to cause injury, pain, or harm

CRITICAL THINKING QUESTIONS

1. Why do you think it's easier to control someone who doesn't know how to read or write?

2. In what ways did Walker help other black women?

3. What did Walker do to try to reduce the amount of violence against black people?

READ MORE

Harrison, Vashti. *Little Leaders: Bold Women in Black History.* New York; Boston, MA: Little, Brown and Company, 2017.

Kirkfield, Vivian. *Sweet Dreams, Sarah.* Berkeley, CA: Creston Books, 2019.

Simons, Lisa M. Bolt. *Madam C.J. Walker: Inventor and Businesswoman.* STEM Scientists and Inventors. North Mankato, MN: Capstone Press, 2018.

INTERNET SITES

Madam C.J. Walker biography
https://www.ducksters.com/biography/entrepreneurs/madamcjwalker.php

The official website of Madam C.J. Walker
http://www.madamcjwalker.com

INDEX